T0096221

OH, CANADIANS!
Hysterically Historical Rhymes

GORDON SNELL

with caricatures by
AISLIN

LITTLE, BROWN CANADA
BOSTON • NEW YORK • TORONTO • LONDON

FIRST PRINTING

Canadian Cataloguing in Publication Data

Snell, Gordon, 1932
Oh, Canadians! Hysterically Historical Rhymes

ISBN 0-316-80313-8

1. Celebrities – Canada – Poetry. 2. Humourous poetry,
English. I. Aislin. II. Title.

PR6069.N4405 1996   821'.914   C96-931411-6

Cover Illustration by *AISLIN*
Cover Design by *AISLIN*
Layout and Design by *MICHAEL P. CALLAGHAN*
Electronic Imaging by *MICHAEL P. CALLAGHAN*
Composed and Set at *MOONS OF JUPITER, INC., TORONTO*
Printed and Bound in Canada by *BEST BOOK MANUFACTURING*

LITTLE, BROWN AND COMPANY (CANADA) LIMITED
148 YORKVILLE AVENUE, TORONTO, ONTARIO, CANADA
M5R 1C2

For all our love and happy times,
To Maeve I dedicate these rhymes.

OH, CANADIANS!

Hysterically Historical Rhymes

The mysterious disappearance
of Sir John Franklin finally
explained...

Contents

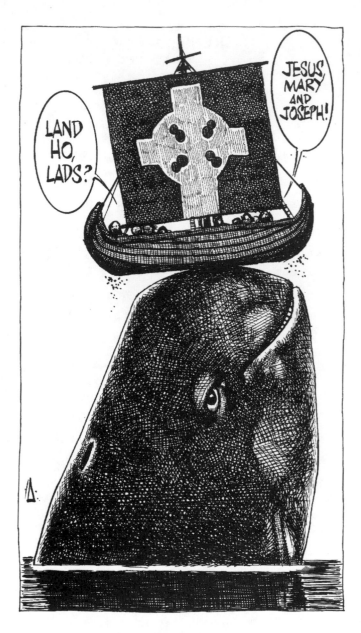

SAINT BRENDAN

SAINT BRENDAN (484 – 578)

Brendan was an Irish monk whose voyages to exotic lands were described in a Latin narrative translated and circulated widely in Europe. Many people believe his journeys took him as far as the American continent.

The Europeans who claim to be
The first, America to see —
Columbus, Cabot, Viking Leif —
May find their claims have come to grief.
There's one who says that First they ain't,
And he is Brendan, Sailor Saint.

That he was real, you can't debunk:
He was a holy Irish monk
Born fifteen centuries ago.
He founded monasteries, we know —
And from a Latin text we learn he
Made the most amazing journey.

Saint Brendan's voyage was designed
The Land of Promise for to find.
He'd dreamed of it, and had, they say,
Bizarre adventures on the way.

They saw upon one island's coasts
Birds that were really hordes of ghosts.
Towards a crystal tower they came,
Then to a mountain, belching flame,

An isle of giants, a curdled sea,
An isle with fruit on every tree;
A rock where Judas had his station,
Let off, on Sundays, from Damnation.

And then they found the boat was beached:
Another isle they must have reached.
But soon the land began to rise:
It was a whale, of giant size.

The boat upon its back was stranded.
The Saint just said: "Well, since we've landed,
This chance we monks must not let pass:
We'll gather round, and say a Mass!"
And when the Mass was done, the whale
Sank down, and Brendan's ship set sail.

The tale's interpretation varies:
Some say he went to the Canaries,
To Iceland, and the Faroes too;
But others take a bolder view:
They say that Brendan's holy band
Went on as far as Newfoundland.

Tim Severin thought so, set afloat
A replica of Brendan's boat,
And though the weather was atrocious
The coast *he* reached was Nova Scotia's!

The day may come when we shall find
Some object Brendan left behind:
A Celtic cross, some rosary beads —
That sort of find is all it needs
To make all other claimants yield
And prove Saint Brendan led the field!

LEIF ERICCSON

LEIF ERICCSON   (died 1020)

According to the Viking sagas, Leif Ericcson crossed the Atlantic, and the lands he visited are probably Baffin Island and Labrador, and finally Vinland, which could be Newfoundland.

The average marauding Viking
Seized any land that took his liking.
No place was safe in early days
From Scandinavian forays.

Eric the Red first got a taste
To settle Greenland's icy waste,
And soon Leif Ericcson, his son,
His own great journeys had begun.

Over a thousand years ago
He was the first, the sagas show,
Who came from European lands
To step upon Canadian strands.
For those who watched those tall prows rise on
The empty, faraway horizon,
They must have made a curious sight
With spears and helmets gleaming bright.

To Baffin Island, where Leif came,
"The Land of Stones" he gave the name.
"The Wooded Land" he called the shore
Of what we know as Labrador.

In "Vinland" next that crew arrived,
And there the winter they survived.
They found there everything they wished:
Good pastures, salmon to be fished,
And even berries, grapes and vines —
That's why Leif called it "Land of Wines."

Though Vinland's written into history,
Its whereabouts is still a mystery.
Some choose Cape Cod, but others say
It's further north, near Hudson Bay;
And others claim they understand
It's on the coast of Newfoundland.

It must have been, if that is so,
Much warmer, centuries ago.
If only it had stayed that way,
We might be all enjoying today
The Newfoundlanders' Chardonnay.

But as it is, they've found their niche
With something stronger: pass the SCREECH!

JOHN CABOT   (1425 – c.1500)

Originally from Italy, John Cabot went to England to get backing from King Henry VII and the merchants of Bristol to search for a sea route to Asia. He was the first of the explorers of that period to land on the North American continent.

For navigators, like John Cabot,
Ocean trips became a habit.
From youth, he heard the waters call —
He was Venetian, after all.

But Bristol merchants, and the King,
Financed John Cabot's journeying.
In 1497, he
Aboard the *Matthew* went to sea.
He reached the coast, we understand,
Most probably in Newfoundland.
In fact, the date he landed on
Was at the feast day of St John.

He raised a flag, in England's name,
Set several snares to capture game,
And said: "Lest anyone forgets,
I'll leave this needle too, for nets —
Then passers-by will be advised
This place is truly colonised."

No doubt the people living there
Were not aware, or didn't care

That he had come to their locality
And claimed to change their nationality!

More vital was the news he bore
Of oceans full of fish galore:
For Cabot on the way had found
The future Grand Banks fishing ground.

Though people praise Columbus more
For *his* trip, just five years before,
That sailor, after many dramas,
Had only got to the Bahamas;
While Cabot, with the same intent,
At least had reached the Continent.

Yet both explorers never ceased
To think that they had reached the East.
They didn't know, like us today,
America was in the way!

JACQUES CARTIER

JACQUES CARTIER   (1491 – 1557)

Jacques Cartier was the first European to explore the Gulf of St. Lawrence and the St. Lawrence River. His encounters with the Iroquois ranged from friendship to hostility, and the treasure he finally brought home was not what he expected.

"Sail west!" Jacques Cartier was told,
"And find me countries rich in gold."
The King of France had spoken, so
Jacques thought he'd really better go.
Besides, it was a mission which
With any luck, would make him rich.

He crossed the ocean, but he found
That Labrador was barren ground.
He treated it with some abhorrence —
But then he came to the St. Lawrence.
He crossed the Gulf, and made his way
Along the coast to Gaspé Bay.

And there he managed to annoy
The friendly local Iroquois
By putting up a giant cross
To show them all just who was Boss.

Chief Donnacona wasn't pleased —
But strained relations soon were eased.
It was Jacques' Gallic charm, we think —
Or was there something in the drink?

At any rate, Jacques took the chance
To ask the Chief's two sons to France.

The next year, when he brought them back,
They helped to put him on the track:
They showed him the St. Lawrence River.
"What riches I can now deliver!"
Exclaimed Jacques Cartier, as they told
Of distant kingdoms, full of gold.

He also thought the river went
Right through into the Orient.
And so, continuing his saga,
He sailed right on, to Hochelaga.

There, he was joyfully received.
He'd cure the sick, they all believed.
He read the Gospel of St John,
And though their pains and aches weren't gone,
They kindly didn't swear and curse:
At least, he hadn't made them worse.

A nearby mountain he did name,
And *Mont-Royal* it then became —
Now Montreal, the very same.
Then winter came, and scurvy too.
No Gospel cured that, Cartier knew.

The Iroquois' white-cedar brew
Was what saved most of Cartier's crew.

No thanks they got, but only grief:
In spring Jacques came and seized their Chief.
He took ten other prisoners too.
"I'll bring them back as good as new!"
That's what he promised, but we know
His vows all melted, with the snow.

To Canada the navigator
Did not return till six years later.
This time, he built a settlement:
To colonize was his intent.
But he was even more delighted
When gold and diamonds were sighted.

He thought that they'd be valued highly
And he would live the life of Riley.
But back in France, he found the ore
Was iron pyrites, nothing more,
And learned from valuers' reports
His diamonds were only quartz.

At least, the jewellers today
Have saved the name of CARTIER!

HENRY HUDSON

HENRY HUDSON   (died 1611)

Henry Hudson, who gave his name to so many places, made four voyages searching for a northern route to the Pacific and China, and was finally cast adrift in an open boat by his rebellious crew.

Henry Hudson several times
Tried to sail to Eastern climes
Searching for the Isles of Spice,
But was always foiled by ice.

People thought the route northeast
Would lead to China at the least,
But up among the Arctic seas
Hudson found not one Chinese.

On the third trip, Hudson's men,
Ice-bound, grumbled: "Not again!"
A mutiny was in the air,
But Hudson fixed them with a glare:
"Well, if you feel like that," he said,
"We'll turn and sail northwest, instead!"
It made the sailors much less frantic,
Sailing over the Atlantic.

Up the Hudson River then
To Albany he took his men,
Thus showing that this waterway
Could be a trading route one day.

"Whatever this new land has got,"
Said Hudson, "China it is not!"

And so next year, in 1610,
Henry Hudson sailed again.
The spicy Orient was beckoning —
From the west, by Hudson's reckoning.

He believed that Davis Strait
Would be the Northwest Passage gate,
And lead him to an Arctic Sea
Which from drifting ice was free.
But the tide, so fierce and great,
Swept him to another Strait:
The one named Hudson, after him —
Though then, his fate was looking grim.

The crew began to rage and curse,
But turning round would just be worse.
Through icy seas they made their way
Four hundred miles, at ten per day,
Emerging into Hudson Bay.
Henry Hudson felt terrific:
He thought he'd entered the Pacific!

So south they sailed, and found James Bay,
Thinking that China lay that way.
Hudson searched for many days

But found the coast was like a maze.
And then there came the winter snows,
And all the land and waters froze.

Although they built a house on shore,
The winter chilled them to the core.
Now and then they caught some game,
But the dreaded scurvy came
And Henry Hudson got the blame.

When the ice broke up, they sailed:
Though the China trip had failed,
Hudson at the least could say
He'd discovered Hudson Bay.

But he never got the chance —
The others looked at him askance,
And what really roused their passions
Was finding Hudson's hidden rations.

After that, he got short shrift:
Rebels cast a boat adrift
With Hudson and eight men on board.
The rest cried: "That is your reward!"

A mystery surrounds the ends
Of Henry Hudson and his friends,
Left in the icy seas to float

In a leaky open boat.
Bligh kept such a group together,
But *he* had rather warmer weather!

Hudson, though, could not survive —
And yet his name remains alive:
The Bay, the Company, the Strait,
And towns and rivers, make him great.
But dying of cold and of starvation,
Great fame is not much consolation.

JAMES WOLFE

JAMES WOLFE (1727 – 1759)

James Wolfe reached the height of his military career in 1759 when he was made commander of the British land forces in the expedition against the French in Quebec. Though the attack succeeded, both he and the French general, Montcalm, died in the battle.

Wolfe started young — at just fourteen,
He first joined up as a Marine.
Perhaps it was coincidence
That out, of all the regiments,
The one that took him in was led
By James's father, at its head.

Marines for Infantry James swapped,
And then his progress never stopped.
He fought in Scotland, Belgium, France,
And then he got his biggest chance.

At Louisbourg he helped attack
The French ships, which were firing back;
He captured some, put some to flame,
And in that battle made his name.
Commander was his next position,
To take Quebec his army's mission.

The French defence force was Montcalm's:
Wolfe faced him without any qualms.
For James, in planning every fight,

Believed that he was always right —
A fact which often, it appears,
Caused quarrels with his Brigadiers.

Wolfe changed his plans throughout that summer:
Some were inspired, some rather dumber.
His main intention, though, was sound:
To tempt Montcalm to open ground.
But that sly General rightly thought:
"My fortress is a safer spot."

At last, and after several tries,
The British troops achieved surprise.
Boats full of soldiers, undetected,
Made landings where they weren't expected.
Beneath the cliffs, at dead of night,
They came ashore, and scaled the height.

Montcalm was now in quite a jam
There on the Plains of Abraham.
His enemy was growing stronger —
He knew that he could wait no longer.

So out he went; some progress made,
The French then met a fusillade.
The furious bombardment stunned them:
British forces had outgunned them.

Montcalm directed a retreat,
But never lived to see defeat:
A fatal bullet struck him down.
Wolfe never saw the captured town —
Although he reached the very portal,
The wounds that he received were mortal.
Quebec surrendered, but the war
Continued for a few years more.

The conquerors in this aggression
Were doubtful of their new possession.
So vast, so troublesome, so cold —
Was this a land they'd *want* to hold?
And some officials seemed to feel
To give it back had more appeal:
The French might think it quite a scoop
To swap the place for Guadeloupe...

And Canada, with that entente,
Would have *une histoire différente!*

JAMES McGILL

JAMES McGILL (1744 – 1813)

James McGill came from Scotland to join the fur trade in Canada. He became a leading merchant and a civic figure in Montreal, where he founded the university that bears his name.

Canada lured lots and lots
Of young and enterprising Scots,
And one from Glasgow felt the call
To come and live in Montreal.
His name is celebrated still:
He was the famous James McGill.

His University, begun
Way back in 1821,
Has nurtured many brilliant students
Of literature, and jurisprudence
For science, too, its classes cater —
In fact, no accolade is greater
Than saying: "McGill's my Alma Mater!"

Glasgow was where James went to college:
He had an early thirst for knowledge
And entered there, so we are told,
When he was only twelve years old.

At twenty-two, he'd emigrated —
In Montreal he was located;
And he was at the Great Lakes too

Dispatching parties by canoe
With *voyageurs* among the crew.

As more canoes like his departed
The northwest fur trade really started;
And in exchange for furs would come
Gunpowder, silver, cloth and rum.

Then as the fur trade grew and grew,
The canny merchants prospered too:
The warehouses on Rue Saint-Paul
Held James's wealth in Montreal.

When, angered by the Quebec Act,
America with troops attacked,
McGill and others made a pact
So Montreal would not be sacked.
Surrender was negotiated
And those invaders were placated.

Though Montreal was occupied,
James would not join the rebel side
And even voiced his detestation
Of this attempt at 'Liberation'.
To show McGill he was mistaken,
His cellar full of rum was taken.

When finally the armies went,
Benjamin Franklin then was sent
With revolutionary intent,
But found that none would heed his call
In French *or* English Montreal.
His journal, though, is with us yet:
It's called the *Montreal Gazette*.

The city prospered — James did too.
His civic reputation grew
And several times a seat he earned
When the Assembly was returned.
But he was not, for all his zest,
Deficient in self-interest.

In fact McGill was most adroit
Acquiring land around Detroit.
When that became a U.S. city,
He may have thought it was a pity,
But he obtained, by obligation,
Canadian lands in compensation.

That made him see it could be grand
To start to speculate in land.
Such enterprises made McGill,
Already wealthy, richer still,
And prompted him to make a will.

With gifts of money and of land
A University he planned,
Where many a future generation
Has owed to him their education;
And there Canadians honour still
The famous name of James McGill.

GEORGE VANCOUVER

GEORGE VANCOUVER   (1757 – 1798)

George Vancouver's first voyages were with Captain Cook, but he is most celebrated for his epic four-and-a-half year journey along the western coast of Canada and the USA, charting over seventy thousand miles of coastline.

George Vancouver took a trip
At fourteen, on a naval ship.
His native England he forsook
To see the world with Captain Cook.
From him he was to learn the arts
Of making perfect maps and charts.

Cook's second trip with George aboard
The northwest coastal shores explored,
And George Vancouver was, what's more,
First European upon that shore.

Then off Cook went, two thousand miles,
To what he called the Sandwich Isles.
It's really hard to know just *why* he
Ignored their proper name, *Hawaii.*

The islanders thought Cook no friend,
And at their hands he met his end.
They nearly killed Vancouver too,
But he escaped with all his crew.

His death then would have been a pity —
For what would we have called the city?
But George lived on, and got promotion,
And sailed for the Pacific Ocean.
There, Spain was causing a commotion:
The coast was theirs, they had a notion.

The British government was furious,
Maintaining that the claim was spurious.
(The people living there, it's true,
Were never asked to give *their* view.)

Then José Martinez's band
Seized lots of British ships and land,
And when he dared to shout "Olé!"
The British cried: "No way, José!"

They needed now a speedy mover,
And so they sent in George Vancouver.
For what the British wanted most
Were surveys, up and down the coast.
"With those," they said, "you can declare
If there's a Northwest Passage there."

Some thought not all the coast was *dry* land —
Perhaps Alaska was an island?
George may have thought such views ridiculous,
But still, his survey was meticulous,
And all his skill and strength he put

Into that mapping, foot by foot.
The narrowest inlets he'd explore
In open boats, to reach the shore.

His survey, he could really boast,
Scanned sixty thousand miles of coast.
The small boats' trips increased the score
By something like ten thousand more.

Four years it took to bring it off —
Then, near the Isle of Baranof
Far to the north, Vancouver anchored
And took the rest for which he hankered.

"We've done it!" was his declaration,
"Get out the grog, in celebration!
And while we have our drinking session
Let's say farewell to one obsession,
The Northwest Passage! We have let it
Rule all our lives, and hope we met it.
Now we can simply say, 'FORGET IT!'
You might as well, to get to China,
Dig out a trench from Carolina."

Was he much wiser than he knew?
Digging a trench is what they'd do.
Southwards, years later, they installed it —
The Panama Canal they called it.

SIR ALEXANDER MACKENZIE

SIR ALEXANDER MACKENZIE
(1764 – 1820)

Alexander Mackenzie was ten when his family emigrated first to New York and then to Canada. He became a fur trader and made two epic journeys west, trekking by canoe and on foot in search of a route to the Pacific.

The search for furs; this was the quest
Which led Mackenzie to the west.
For there, the wilderness was rife
With every kind of furry life:
Beavers and otters, foxes, minks,
The wolf, the marten and the lynx.

They all made fashionable furs
And classy headgear, His and Hers.
For then the fur trade went unchecked,
Though not politically correct.
Creatures were killed without apology,
And no one cared about ecology.

The Athabasca River ran
Beside the new Fort Chipewyan,
And here Mackenzie's trek began.
With just twelve men in three canoes,
Slave River was the route he'd choose.
Off to the west they paddled forth,
Then found the river heading north.

Mackenzie wouldn't be downcast:
They paddled on, and paddled fast.
One hundred miles a day they went,
To reach the ocean their intent.
When finally they saw the sea,
All frozen it appeared to be.

Mackenzie grumbled: "What a shame!
This river here by which we came,
Let Disappointment be its name."
But others thought that name too grim,
And later named it after *him*.

His colleagues in the trade, however,
Were not impressed by his endeavour.
They said: "A sea of ice won't suit
As any kind of trading route."
Mackenzie though was resolute,
And four years later, with nine men
And one dog, he set out again.

Peace River was the way to go,
But did they find it peaceful? No!
Mackenzie and his nine companions
Faced rapids and cascades and canyons,
Hauled the canoe and all their goods
Up rocky paths through gloomy woods;
Midst snowy mountains, never warm,
They camped, and sheltered from a storm.

Mackenzie took the chance to write
Of all they'd done until that night,
Then in an empty rum keg placed
His diary of the route they'd traced
And all the dangers they had faced.

He cast the keg into the river
And hoped his note it would deliver.
The postal service now is better —
Then, it was chancier... and wetter!

For weeks Mackenzie and his team
Went bravely struggling upstream,
And wondered, was it all a dream?
Perhaps, although they'd done their best,
There *was* no river to the West.

But then they met a local guide
Who led them to the Great Divide.
And west from here, they had a notion,
Lay the great Pacific Ocean.
But soon, by icy waters battered,
Their lone canoe was nearly shattered:
Instead of paddling, as they planned,
They had to journey overland.

They found a river, guides who knew
This land where giant cedars grew,

And villages where they would dine
On salmon, deer, and porcupine.

But further on, the records tell us,
They met the warlike Bella Bellas
And found them much less friendly fellas.

An angry warrior climbed aboard
And grabbed Mackenzie's gun and sword,
And said white men, a few weeks back,
Had used such weapons to attack.
(The story that he told was true:
It was Vancouver and his crew.)

Back in his own canoe once more,
"Follow!" they heard the warrior roar.
Instead, they raced towards the shore;
They climbed a rock, and on the top
There for the night they had to stop.

Next day, as soon as it was light,
Two war canoes came into sight:
The outlook wasn't very bright.
And yet Mackenzie showed no fear —
He said: "Before we disappear,
The world must know that I was here!"

He wrote a record of his visit —
Like Kilroy, only more explicit:

Upon the rock, in letters great,
He scrawled his own name, and the date.
He wrote too, so they'd understand,
He'd come from Canada, by land.

The others neither groused nor brooded
To see *their* names were not included,
For they were more concerned that day
With how to make their getaway.

The warriors' canoes gave chase
But finally they lost the race;
Yet still Mackenzie had to face
The cruel journey back to base.
Somehow, the party made their way
At nearly forty miles a day,
And Alexander gained much glory
By later publishing his story.

Among the readers, for a start,
There was Napoleon Bonaparte:
He planned to beat the British back
With a Canadian attack.

Back home, the King did not demur,
But promptly dubbed Mackenzie "Sir".
Which shows what marvels can occur
From starting out to search for fur!

The mysterious disappearance of Sir John Franklin finally explained...

SIR JOHN FRANKLIN

SIR JOHN FRANKLIN   (1786 – 1847)

John Franklin was a naval officer who charted thousands of miles of Canada's Arctic coast in the quest for the Northwest Passage. He made four expeditions and met his death during the last one.

King William Island's frozen ground
Was where John Franklin's corpse was found,
His bones the only indication
Of that brave life of exploration.

From age fourteen, his naval life
Was filled with roving and with strife.
Then, Franklin saw his true vocation
In Canadian exploration.

The powers-that-be were all obsessed
With finding routes from east to west.
They sought the Northwest Passage which
Would help make everybody rich.

Franklin's first journey had no luck:
In polar ice they nearly stuck.
The second time from Hudson Bay
To Yellowknife he made his way,
Then down the river Coppermine —
The prospect, though, was far from fine.

Sometimes a frozen lake they crossed,
Their faces bitten by the frost.
Canoes on pairs of sleds were put:
Dogs dragged them, while men walked on foot.
The ice was honeycombed by rain,
And jagged edges caused great pain.
The men's and dogs' feet, when they bled,
Left on the ice a trail of red.

The journey seemed to take them ages,
And Franklin fumed with frequent rages.
No wonder that the Inuit feared
This sullen group, and disappeared.
And so, without the Inuits' aid,
The two canoes their journey made,
And for a month the coast surveyed.

Then food got short, and tempers too,
And murmurs of rebellion grew.
It wasn't long before John Franklin
Sensed grudges and resentments ranklin'.
He said: "We must return, it's plain:
I'll name this Point here Turnagain."
The men said: "Call it what you like —
But turn around, or we shall strike!"

They had no food, and their canoes
Were damaged far too much to use.

So overland the route they tried.
Frozen and starving, nine men died.
The rest, in order to survive,
Ate lichen just to keep alive.
A local tribe who knew the place
Found them, and brought them back to base.

Now, Franklin was a famous name;
And though a hero he became,
He found that life at home was boring,
And yearned again to go exploring.
Better equipped, he mapped once more
Hundreds of miles of Arctic shore.

Then late in life he got the chance
To make the final great advance.

Three hundred miles remained uncharted:
So for the Arctic coast he started —
But not before he watched them stowing
Three years' supplies to keep them going.
Steam boilers drove propellers, too,
And heated pipes to warm the crew.
A library of books was there,
And wine, cut-glass, and silverware.

In 1845, in May,
The ships sailed out to Baffin Bay.

But no one knew what happened then
To Franklin and his ships and men.
In that white world, so wild and weird,
They had completely disappeared.

The years passed — forty expeditions
Went sailing out on searching missions.
And Franklin's widow did her best
To press for yet another quest.
When she had waited fourteen years,
A gruesome find confirmed her fears.

King William Island was the site
Where Franklin's body came to light:
Two skeletons, one his, they guessed
From silver spoons that bore his crest.

The Northwest Passage now was mapped,
And in its icy wastes were trapped
Many explorers' ships and crews
Whose families had received no news
Of how they suffered and they died,
Unknown and unidentified.

At least they found John Franklin's grave —
A stern explorer, rash and brave:
For charts and maps his life he gave.

Though Europeans' success was heady,
The Inuit knew that coast already;
If Franklin with his dedication
Had sought out their co-operation,
He might have saved the situation.

WILLIAM LYON MACKENZIE

WILLIAM LYON MACKENZIE
(1795 – 1861)

A journalist and a politician, Mackenzie was a tireless and fierce advocate of reform. As a member of Upper Canada's Assembly, he was expelled and re-elected many times, and became the first mayor of Toronto. In 1837 he led an unsuccessful rebellion, fled to the U.S.A,, was jailed, and then returned after an amnesty to further turbulent years in Canadian politics.

The mind of William Lyon Mackenzie
Was in a state of constant frenzy.
When Tory values were the norm,
He preached political reform.

He started, to promote his aims,
Papers with many different names.
When one would fail, he wasn't vexed:
He'd bounce right back and start the next.

In Upper Canada's Assembly
Mackenzie's foes were all a-trembly.
He lashed the opposition ranks
And even criticised the Banks —
An attitude, which some might say,
Would also find support today...

He was elected, then rejected,
And then once more was re-elected.
In such esteem the people held him

That when his enemies expelled him
A crowd of several hundred went
And marched right into Parliament.
And after that the by-election
Made him the popular selection.

Then Yonge Street rang with cheers of praise,
As bagpipes and a hundred sleighs
Went in a great procession, led
By William, riding at the head.

Yet still his foes, infuriated,
Kept booting out the man they hated —
But he was always re-instated.
He said: "If this goes on much more,
I'll ask for a revolving door!"

Now when Toronto first was founded,
Up to new heights Mackenzie bounded.
The brand new Council then and there
Made William Lyon Mackenzie mayor.
But in provincial politics
He couldn't beat the Governor's tricks:
That ruling agent of the Crown
Kept putting the reformers down.

Mackenzie now began devising
A plan to stage an armed uprising.
He wrote, to fuel the demonstration,

An Independence Declaration,
And made, to gather his supporters,
Montgomery's Tavern his headquarters.
They prepared to sally forth, "Best
Take Toronto from the west."

Thursday was meant to be the day
When they would all be on their way,
But someone gave the city warning
And so they marched on Tuesday morning.
Then by the Guards with bullets spattered,
Mackenzie's rebel army scattered.

Though further reinforcements then
Came to increase Mackenzie's men,
The city's soldiers came to meet them
And swiftly managed to defeat them.

Mackenzie fled, the battle lost —
Niagara's River then he crossed,
And soon on Navy Island there
Americans arrived to share
As volunteers, with his persuasion,
A plan for Canada's invasion.

They were bombarded from the bank
And then their main supply ship sank,
And soon the U.S. Government
Decided it was time they went.

For William, prosecution waited:
Neutrality he'd violated.
Released on bail, not beaten yet,
He started up a new Gazette,
And wrote, with somewhat rash intent,
Attacks upon the President.

Jailed for a year, he then was pardoned,
And soon his attitudes had hardened.
Back home in Canada once more,
A lot of things made William sore.
He lashed old colleagues, and old laws —
A rebel upon every cause.
He was a man of great panache,
Eccentric, maverick and rash.

Our parties might have more appeal
With some of his reforming zeal.

BLONDIN

CHARLES BLONDIN   (1824 – 1897)

Blondin was from a circus family and became world-famous for his spectacular stunts, particularly his tightrope walks across Niagara Falls.

Blondin, soon after he could talk,
Was learning how to tightrope-walk.
His father knew what he was at:
He was a famous acrobat.

So Blondin felt the great delights
Of prancing round at heady heights.
One day he cried: "Adventure calls —
I'll walk across Niagara Falls!"
And so in 1859,
Blondin prepared to toe the line.

The foaming river stretched out wide —
One thousand feet from side to side.
One slip, and plunging he would go
Into the torrent down below.

The crowd gasped as he took his pole
And started for his distant goal,
With dainty steps, precise and slow,
And not a trace of vertigo.

In twenty minutes, and no more,
He stepped upon the further shore.

The cheering and the shouting drowned
Even the gushing water's sound.

He'd crossed the Falls, and didn't drop —
And after that he wouldn't stop.
Each time he saw a chance, he'd grab it:
He simply couldn't kick the habit.

Blindfold he crossed, straight as an arrow;
Then on the rope he wheeled a barrow.
He crossed with someone on his back,
And with his feet inside a sack.

And then he took a stove along
And watched by the admiring throng
He cooked an omelette in mid-air
And calmly ate it, then and there.
He savoured it, and didn't gobble,
And never made a single wobble.

Through all his great Niagara stunts,
He never put a foot wrong once.
He did things no one else would try,
And just kept walking — high, and dry.
Though people thought he'd soon be dead,
He died at seventy-three — in bed.

SIR SANDFORD FLEMING

SIR SANDFORD FLEMING
(1827 – 1915)

As a railway engineer, Sandford Fleming helped to build the new railroads across Canada. He invented the international system of Time Zones still used today.

Many good results are stemming
From the work of Sandford Fleming:
Railways, time zones, maps and charts,
Aid for science and the arts,
Progress all across the land
Was helped by Fleming's guiding hand.

An engineer and a surveyor,
He soon became a major player
Among the ranks of those who pressed
For a railroad east to west.

In Newfoundland, and on the plains,
He planned the tracks to take the trains.
Up in the Rockies fierce disputes
Flared up about the likely routes,
But Fleming was a pioneer
Who liked to get his way, it's clear —
And, well — he *was* Chief Engineer!

Soon, trains across the land would hurry —
But Sandford Fleming had a worry.
He'd rush to catch a train, and miss it,

And curse in language most explicit;
With rage he made his protests vocal:
"The time we keep is too damned *local!*"

For way back then, each township said:
"At noon, the sun's straight overhead."
So when Quebec said: "It's noon, pronto!"
"Eleven-thirty!" said Toronto.
This caused rail travellers some vexation,
Changing their watches at each station.

So Fleming then said: "How sublime
If we could have a Standard Time.
A twenty-four hour clock we need,
Which even idiots can read.
The world we should divide, what's more,
In Time Zones, making twenty-four.
On every clock, one time is shown
Until you reach another zone."

Both here and in the U.S.A.
The railway managers said: "Hey!
We do believe you've shown the way."

But others said that Fleming's scheme
Was just another crackpot's dream;
And some declared his plans so flighty
They even flouted God Almighty.

These zealots never stopped condemning
The sinful ways of Sandford Fleming.

It took some years of arguments
Till scientists and governments
Agreed that Fleming's plan made sense.
In 1884 they opted
For Standard Time to be adopted.
So Fleming was triumphant then —
And never missed a train again.

That wasn't all, by any means:
He was the Chancellor of Queen's,
And back in 1851,
When postage stamps were first begun,
He drew the first Canadian one.

He helped to make Canadians able
To reach Australia by cable,
And when he'd nothing else to do
He even wrote a prayer book too.

No wonder people were delighted
When he, aged seventy, was knighted.
Perhaps when honoured by the Queen
She asked the time, and he was seen
To say: "Which Time Zone do you mean?"

A nod to Fleming is a must
For travellers, however fussed,
Each time their watches they adjust.

CALIXA LAVALLÉE

CALIXA LAVALLÉE   (1842 – 1891)

Calixa Lavallée grew up in a musical family, and became a celebrated performer, as well as the composer of Canada's national anthem.

Calixa was a gifted boy —
He was his parents' pride and joy.
His father taught him all he knew:
The violin, and organ too.
His piano-playing was first-rate —
And all this, by the age of eight!

And when he moved to Montreal
His playing really stunned them all.
And then, still in his early teens,
He took a trip to New Orleans
And there he won a competition.
He met another star musician
And off on tour the pair did go
Down to Brazil and Mexico.

This roving life he found so grand,
He joined the Union Army Band,
And got a wound, in Maryland.

He lived in Boston for a spell
And taught there, and performed as well.
He even wrote an opera too,
Which had the title T.I.Q.
He said it meant *The Indian Question*.

To settle it, was his suggestion.
To think his music might achieve
That end was just a bit naïve.

Then back in Canada once more,
A great occasion lay in store:
A Governor-General's installation
Required a musical sensation.
Lavallée was the man they chose
A fine cantata to compose.

He trained a choir with soloists
And many instrumentalists.
The show was lavish and expensive,
The praise was fervent and extensive.

Calixa, though, near lost his senses:
They wouldn't pay him his expenses!

He got the chance, though, one year later
For a performance even greater.
The Société St. Jean-Baptiste
Was holding a gigantic feast:
To celebrate, was their intention,
A French-Canadian convention.

They said: "We need a national song:
With Lavallée, we can't go wrong.
So with *O Canada* we'll show 'em —

Look up the words now, of the poem.
Calixa said: "No need — I know 'em."

He had it finished very soon,
And so was born the national tune.
A massive choir three thousand strong
Gave voice to the composer's song;
Three bands were playing, and the crowd
All clapped and cheered it long and loud.

And soon at every hall and stage
O Canada was all the rage.
It topped, whenever it was played,
The 1880's Hit Parade.
And then it wasn't very long
Before the nation knew the song.

Wherever it is sung today,
Canadians here or far away
Honour Calixa Lavallée:
O Canada is here to stay.

ALEXANDER GRAHAM BELL

ALEXANDER GRAHAM BELL
(1847 – 1922)

Bell was born in Scotland and moved to Canada with his parents in 1870. His lifelong interest was teaching the deaf to speak, but he was a brilliant inventor: a pioneer not only of the telephone, but of sound recording, sonar detection, hydrofoils, and flying machines.

Alexander Graham Bell,
His parents thought, was far from well.
So they decided they would go
To Brantford, in Ontario..
Once there, his health improved immensely,
And he began to work intensely.

Enthusiastically he'd teach
His father's system, *Visible Speech.*
The symbols, which were quite unique,
Could help the deaf to learn to speak.

And meanwhile Bell pursued with zest
Another scientific quest.
For it was one of his desires
To send speech by electric wires.
Thus he believed we could, one day,
Converse with people far away.

The telephone was in the offing —
Which didn't stop the people scoffing.
To make words carry, *they'd* no doubt

The only thing to do was shout!
And when they heard what Bell was after,
They simply doubled up with laughter.

But Bell and Watson, his assistant,
Remained courageous and persistent,
And in their workshop day and night
They toiled to prove that they were right.

Watson one night heard Bell's voice call —
It wasn't coming through the wall,
But down the wires, to Watson's ear:
"Please come here, Watson!" loud and clear.
Watson rushed in to tell his mentor:
"You sure are one great inventor!"

Bell got his patent applications
For his "electric undulations",
And very soon he got the chance
To make a really great advance.

From Tutela Heights his voice would go
To Paris, in Ontario.
And later, when he made a call
To greet his friends in Montreal,
They all cried, when they heard him speak:
"Le Téléphone — c'est magnifique!"

But then, big telegraphic firms
Boldly infringed the patent's terms;
To back his claim, Bell did resort
To lengthy battles through the court.

His company, Bell Telephone,
Was internationally known,
But Bell's resolve was unrelenting:
He just went on and on inventing.

He sent sound down a beam of light
And made experiments with flight,
Like an enormous man-powered kite;
And as these craft got off the ground,
Bell pioneered recorded sound.

Today, he would approve when shown
The wonders of the mobile phone —
But would he really wish to toast
The chatty radio phone-in host?

Or would he feel that each invention
Has some effects too brash to mention?
Such outcomes he could hardly know
Of that first call, so long ago,
At Brantford, in Ontario.

EMMA ALBANI

EMMA ALBANI   (1847 – 1930)

Emma Albani from Montreal became an international opera star, but still maintained her popularity at home, where she was known as Canada's 'Queen of Song'.

Just who was Marie Lajeunesse?
An operatic star, no less.
But when she sought the road to fame,
Like many stars, she changed her name:
EMMA ALBANI she became.

In childhood, she had learned the art:
Her teacher praised her from the start,
Where she grew up, in Montreal.
(He was her father, after all.)

They moved when she was seventeen
To Albany, a whole new scene:
That's why she later thought it witty
To take her stage name from that city.
The spelling, also rather wittily,
Made people think she came from Italy.

There, in the theatre at Messina,
She made her debut, as Amina:
La Sonnambula was her break —
The audience, though, stayed wide awake.

The same role made her all the rage
Upon the Covent Garden stage;
She then, with her career begun,
Married the theatre owner's son.
Apart from all his style and charm,
The move did her career no harm.

And there, for twenty years and more,
Her voice made audiences roar,
And cry out: "Bravo!" and "Encore!"

New Wagner operas she was in,
Like *Tannhauser* and *Lohengrin*.
She sang in New York, at the Met —
Just how prestigious can you get?
And there for Verdi, lucky fellow,
Albani premiered *Otello*.

Although on world-wide tours she'd roam,
She made her theme song *Home Sweet Home.*
And here at home, she was the toast
Of countless fans, from coast to coast.
With bands and fireworks, crowds would throng
To hear the nation's 'Queen of Song'.

This pleased her most, although our star
Sang for the Kaiser and the Tsar,
And caused a lot of royal euphoria

When she performed for Queen Victoria.
And later, honouring her name,
King George the Fifth made her a Dame.

At her farewell, the Albert Hall
Gave many a cheer and curtain call.
She'd come a long way, after all,
This little girl from Montreal.

JAMES NAISMITH

JAMES NAISMITH

James Naismith, from Almonte, Ontario, gained a doctorate in theology in Montreal, He became a gymnastics teacher and inspired his students by inventing the modern game of basketball.

James Naismith studied at McGill:
Theology was *his* great skill.

But then, instead of being a preacher,
He worked as a gymnastics teacher.
And in that role, in Springfield, Mass.,
His greatest triumph came to pass.
There clever James amazed them all
When he invented basketball.

Lessons in his gymnasium
Had left his students feeling glum:
Some new game he must now devise
To make them *want* to exercise.

The janitor he then beseeches:
"Those baskets there, which carry peaches —
Please get me two of them, my friend,
And nail them up, at either end.
And when they're hanging on the wall
Then bring me, please, a soccer ball."

The janitor knew his propensity
For doing things with mad intensity —
And so he did what James requested
And soon this brand-new game was tested.

Although the students cried: "What fun!"
The score was only Nought to One.
They soon improved upon that figure,
And with each game the scores grew bigger.

This didn't please the janitor,
For after each and every score
The ball was trapped — he couldn't leave it,
But had to climb up and retrieve it.
He chuckled when the players fumbled,
But every time they scored, he grumbled.

He said: "Why was this game invented?
Those baskets have me quite demented.
I'm sorry now I ever got 'em:
Why don't I just cut off the bottom?"
He did, and Naismith with a whoop
Cried: "Great! Let's call the thing a hoop!"

The sport took off, and grew in fame —
But still it hadn't got a name.
The students said: "What we must do
Is call this new game after *you*. "

But James, being modest, thought it plain
That that would be a little vain.
It's just as well, for after all,
Who'd play a game called NAISMITHBALL?

STEPHEN LEACOCK

STEPHEN LEACOCK
(1869 – 1944)

Stephen Leacock was one of the leading political economists of his time, and combined this profession with a satirical wit that made him a celebrated literary figure in Canada, the United States and Europe.

Stephen Leacock got a thrill
From years of teaching at McGill.
He taught Political Economy
With really quite unusual bonhomie.
For, expert as he was in money,
He also was extremely funny.

Stephen was one of nature's wits
And had his audience in fits.
Today, as well as Economics,
He'd be among the stand-up comics.

His articles and stories too
Gave him a fame which grew and grew,
Till Stephen Leacock was the toast
Of countless fans from coast to coast.

So lots of money came his way,
And he himself was heard to say:
"My bread, upon the waters cast,
Came back to me as cake, at last!"

He is a type that's sorely missed —
A humorous economist.
Economists have got more numerous,
But would that *one* of them was humorous!

L.M. MONTGOMERY

LUCY MAUD MONTGOMERY
(1874 – 1942)

*The author of the celebrated children's book, "Anne of Green Gables",
was born on Prince Edward Island, where the book is set. She grew up
there with her grandparents, and only left when she married in 1911 and
moved to Ontario, where she continued to write more "Anne" stories.*

At four years old, in church one day,
Maud asked her aunt where Heaven lay.
She pointed upwards — Maud, ecstatic,
Assumed that it was in the attic.
In future, in whatever station,
She was less sure of its location.

She felt, when she was only nine,
That literature should be her line.
A blank verse poem she began;
Her father, not a tactful man,
Read it and said, as Maud's heart sank,
"You're right, my dear, it's *very* blank!"

Prince Edward Island was their home,
Although Maud's father liked to roam,
And several businesses did spawn
Way over in Saskatchewan.

His wife had died when Maud was two,
And so with grandparents she grew,
Upon a farm in Cavendish —
As fine a place as she could wish.

Its beauties, rural and inviting,
Were later to inspire her writing.

Grown up, she taught, and also wrote —
At 6 a.m., wrapped in a coat.
Her first paid work was to be seen
By readers of a magazine:
Verses for which her recompense
Was garden seeds, worth fifty cents.

A newspaper in Halifax
Gave her a job like any hack's:
Society columns, Tea-Time Chat,
Which she was very skilful at.
But all the time she was aspirin'
To be another Keats or Byron.

And then she wrote a novel which,
To her amazement, struck it rich.
Anne of Green Gables was the name
That launched her into wealth and fame.
It told how Anne the orphan came
To join the Cuthberts, at eleven,
And found Prince Edward Island heaven.

Anne's chattering ways, her wild elation,
Her passionate imagination,
Her eager schemes, her tough resilience,
Would bring her readers by the millions.

Though some reviewers made Maud sore —
(The <u>New York Times</u> called "Anne" *a bore*) —
The rest were most enthusiastic,
And Mark Twain thought the book fantastic.

Then a new life for Maud began,
With marriage to a clergyman.
She was a mother and a wife
And lived a calm, church-centred life.
Although she did it very well
She missed Prince Edward Island's spell,
And visits there would always be
A journey into memory.

Meanwhile, her readers all desired
More of the girl they so admired.
Anne of Green Gables was adored:
"Give us more stories!" they implored.

These Maud Montgomery supplied,
Though wearily she sometimes sighed:
"I wish that I could turn the tables,
And close the shutters on Green Gables!"

But still more fame would come her way:
There were two movies, and a play —
Yet Anne's creator got no pay.
Her contract, though she reached the heights,
Had never mentioned movie rights!

And now, though Maud herself is gone,
Her sparky heroine lives on,
And visitors from many lands
See where the house Green Gables stands.

And maybe, since she took the view
Reincarnation could be true,
Does Maud Montgomery see it too?

ROBERT. W. SERVICE

ROBERT W. SERVICE
– and those who came after him...   (1874 – 1958)

Robert Service's boisterous ballads about characters like Dangerous Dan McGrew earned him huge popularity as the Bard of the Yukon. He arrived from Scotland as a young man, and after years of roving he became a bank clerk in Whitehorse and Dawson City soon after the great Gold Rush days.

The life of Robert W. Service
Would make most normal people nervous.
His journeys through the frozen wastes
Were not to everybody's tastes —
But though in life they'd do without them,
They simply loved to read about them,
And with his books he was, henceforth,
The Bard of the Canadian North.

Brought up in Scotland, as a lad
A taste for verse he always had,
And on his poetry he'd work,
When in the bank he was a clerk.
When done with debtors and with creditors,
He'd send his poems off to editors,
Who published his poetic flights
In *People's Friend* and *Scottish Nights*.

Then of the banking life he tired:
By wanderlust he was inspired.
Young Robert said he couldn't wait

To board a ship and emigrate.
With joy he stood upon the deck
To watch the docking at Quebec.
He had a ticket to the west
And just five dollars in his vest.

The crowded train moved down the track —
He slept upon the luggage rack;
And on that journey he was quite
A striking, if a curious, sight.
For he was dressed like Buffalo Bill:
His feet high circus-boots did fill,
And on his head, so debonair-o,
He wore a dashing black sombrero.

Fine, if in movies he'd appeared —
In Winnipeg he just looked weird.

But as the train went on and on
Most of his gear was quickly gone.
He had to sell things, one by one:
His suit, his camera, his gun.

Yet on the Rockies as he gazed
He felt ecstatic and amazed.
To a Pacific dawn he woke
Elated, eloquent, and broke.

And so his wandering life began:
He was a farm hand, dairyman,
An orange picker, lumberjack,
Dug tunnels for a trolley track,
Became a hobo and a bum,
Slept on the ground, his cold limbs numb;
At farm doors tried to cadge a meal,
And even chewed banana peel.

In bunks he felt the bed bugs bite,
And in his notebooks tried to write.
His mates found this a bit dismaying,
But they enjoyed his banjo playing.

He finally rejoined the ranks
Of humble clerks who toil in banks;
And soon they said, to Robert's joy:
"You're going to the Yukon, boy!"

By boat to Skagway, then by rail,
He followed that old Gold Rush Trail.
In Whitehorse for three years he stayed —
The brightest move he ever made.

For there, the gateway to the North,
Sourdoughs to him their tales poured forth
Of Gold Rush Times, of bar-room fights,
Of gaudy, bawdy days and nights,

Of booze and broads, ferocious feuds,
Grafters and gamblers and dudes,
Of gold dust gleaming in the pan
And Mounties, out to get their man,
Of strange things done in the midnight sun
—And Robert noted every one.

He noted too, with style and grace,
The wild, white beauty of the place.
He'd walk on snowshoes through the night,
The far, cold moon his only light;
And as he walked with quiet tread
The verses came into his head.

Soon Dan McGrew had been created
And frozen Sam McGee cremated;
But in a cupboard, put away,
They didn't see the light of day.
At last he thought: "This makes no sense —
I'll publish, at my own expense."

The publisher sent back his money;
"Your verse," he said, "is fine and funny!"
So out that first slim volume came:
Songs of a Sourdough was its name.
It brought its author instant fame —
And fortune, for the writing game
Earned more than many a Gold Rush claim.

But Robert was a thrifty feller —
He kept his bank job as a teller.
To Dawson City he transferred;
The Klondike too his name had heard.
His new mates, bowing to his skill,
Cried: "Here's the Bard of Bawdyville!"

And in the mess, that bunch of boys
Would whoop it up with so much noise
That Robert then could only write
Well after midnight every night.

He left the bank and closed his till,
But, keen to stay in Dawson still,
He found a cabin on a hill.
There, walking he would often go
At seventy-two degrees below,
With icicles upon his breath
And danger of a frostbite death.

There, washing sometimes wasn't nice,
Rubbing down with chunks of ice.
Yet Robert Service thought it great,
And wrote *The Trail of '98*.

For many years he wrote his tales,
Long after he had left those trails.
And in those Klondike tales he told,
He truly struck a vein of gold.

Those characters delight us still:
There's Chewed-Ear Jenkins, Barb-Wire Bill,
And all that brash and boisterous crew:
The Ragtime Kid, and Dan McGrew,
And Sam McGee who warmed right through,
And, of course, the Lady known as Lou.

Though long before these fine creations,
The living culture of First Nations
Had viewed this land with subtle eyes
And shaped their arts to match its size,
Woven webs of songs and stories
Harmonized with all its glories.

Service was first to use with pride
The English language, versified,
To conjure up with joy and zest
The wild ways of his new-found West.

Since then, Canadians present
A literary firmament,
Where John McRae his talent wields
While poppies grow in Flanders Fields,
And Leacock, the economist,
Becomes a famous humorist.

Before him, Haliburton came:
His *Clockmaker*, Sam Slick by name,

Gained international acclaim.
While Pauline Johnson got together
Her poetry, in *Flint and Feather*,
And Lucy Maud Montgomery's *Anne*
Her sparkling careeer began.

Later, novelists arose
Whose names now everybody knows.
Robertson Davies earned high praise
With essays, stories, books and plays,
And the tales of Margaret Laurence
Brought her praise in mighty torrents.

Mordecai Richler, most provoking,
Makes people ask how much he's joking.
And lively too was the arrival
Of Margaret Atwood's book, *Survival*.
Her verse and novels are a hit
In all Canadian English Lit.
When she describes the bush, we find
She also maps the human mind.

Alice Munro touches our hearts
With all her storyteller's arts.
Michael Ondaatje never shirks
Delving where myth or marvel lurks,
And Farley Mowat's loved, it's clear,
Not just by *People of the Deer*.

MARGARET ATWOOD

For Carol Shields, no honour fits her
Better than prizes like Pulitzer:
That's where her fine *Stone Diaries* took her —
And it was listed for the Booker!

The reading public too are certain
To hail the works of Pierre Berton.
To *The Last Spike* he never fails
To keep the show upon the rails.

The list of works and those who write 'em
Goes on and on, ad infinitum,
Too rich and vast to classify
(Unless of course you're Northrop Frye) —
Which shows the future's safe and sure
For good Canadian literature,
So full of power and wit and radiance —
Here's to all literary Canadians!

MACK SENNETT *(1880 – 1960)*

Mack Sennett, the pioneer of silent film comedy and creator of the Keystone Cops, was born and grew up in Quebec. After stage work as a chorus boy and vaudeville artist, he went into movies, and began his celebrated career as actor and director.

"My name," said actor Michael Sinnott,
"Has really got no glamour in it."
Did it have more, one wonders, when it
Was altered to become MACK SENNETT?

Born in Quebec when times were tough,
He knocked around, lived fast and rough,
And then decided that the thing
He'd really like to do was sing.

But he got little fame or joy
Performing as a chorus boy,
Though he acquired some comic skill
In burlesque shows and vaudeville.

At movies then he had a go;
Producers didn't shout: "Bravo!"
And snubbed him with: "We'll let you know."
Sennett was not discouraged, though,
And still hung round the studio.

Eventually he got a role
In Griffith's film, *The Curtain Pole*.

The curtain rose on his career,
And Sennett's screen success was clear.

Soon he was one of Griffith's troupe,
With Mary Pickford in the group.
D. W. Griffith would select
Mack Sennett also to direct.

And then he made a great advance:
Two bookmakers took quite a chance,
Deciding they'd provide finance.
And that was the inauguration
Of Keystone Pictures Corporation.

Soon Sennett's comedies were tops,
Especially the Keystone Cops.
The audiences clapped and cheered
When that fantastic Force appeared.

By crafty crooks those Cops were goaded,
Trains ran them down, and cars exploded.
In wild pursuits and hectic chases
The custard pies festooned their faces.
Those flickering reels of celluloid
Had audiences overjoyed.

While policemen did their slapstick duties,
Mack also filmed his Bathing Beauties,

A line of girls with twinkling eyes
And costumes draping wiggling thighs.
Though, seeing today how stars divest,
Mack Sennett's belles look overdressed.

Of all the Beauties in Mack's stable
His best and greatest love was Mabel.
Sennett, for all his comic antics,
Was truly one of life's romantics,
And Mabel Normand was by far,
In films and life, his brightest star.

So many great careers would grow
From Sennett's Keystone Studio.
The young Charles Chaplin started there;
He spotted, too, Frank Capra's flair.

There Gloria Swanson got her chance,
And Harry Langdon he'd advance.
Bing Crosby starred there for a spell,
And Fatty Arbuckle as well.
Though once they all were up and started
To other studios they departed.

When talkies came, so cheered and fêted,
Mack Sennett's style looked rather dated.
His comedies seemed far less funny,
And soon poor Mack lost all his money.

He said farewell to Hollywood,
But couldn't part from it for good.
Though some might think him on the shelf,
In several films he played himself.

When honoured by the Film Academy,
He said: "Well, *they* can't think so bad o' me!"
And *Hollywood Cavalcade* would be
Mack Sennett's film biography.

A stage show honours him as well:
His tale's a splendid one to tell,
For he had played a major part
In shaping cinematic art.

The boy who started in Quebec
To Hollywood had made the trek,
And in that silent era he
Became the King of Comedy.

His Keystone Cops remain immortal
Wherever audiences chortle
At custard pies and slapstick farces,
And policemen falling on their arses.

MARY PICKFORD

MARY PICKFORD (1893 – 1979)

Mary Pickford was a flourishing child actress on the Canadian stage until she went first to Broadway and then into movies, becoming one of the most idolized stars of the silent screen.

Born in Toronto, Gladys Smith
Became a cinematic myth.
The glamorous Gladys rose to fame
With Mary Pickford as her name.

When she was three, her father died.
"How shall we live?" her mother sighed.
And then at five, on theatre stages,
Young Gladys started earning wages.

The child star flourished — at fourteen
She entered on the Broadway scene.
Though in some films she'd take a part,
She felt that it demeaned her art.

D. W. Griffith was the man
With whom her film career began.
He was a most perceptive fella:
He picked her out for *Cinderella*.

Such waif-like roles there were aplenty:
Poor Little Rich Girl, Sweet and Twenty,
Oh, Uncle! and *The Little Teacher* —
In countless films did Mary feature.

In all her winsome, child-like parts
She broke the audiences' hearts.
And very soon, with growing fame,
The national Sweetheart she became.

But though her roles were coy and cute,
Her business sense was most astute.
She and her mother, it would seem,
Made up a great financial team.
Their entry to negotiations
Gave movie moguls palpitations.

From forty dollars every week,
Much higher earnings she would seek.
In just two years they sure got bigger:
Ten thousand weekly was the figure!

She was among the first to see
A star could ask a massive fee
And make the Studios agree.

The moguls couldn't win the fight:
It took, to get her contract right,
According to Sam Goldwyn's stricture,
Much longer than to make the picture!

In 1919, stars she knew —
Fairbanks and Chaplin, Griffith too —

With Mary thought they'd have a go
At forming their own Studio.

United Artists had appeared:
The movie moguls scoffed and sneered.
"The lunatics" — as one did style 'em —
"Have taken over the asylum!"

Mary and Douglas Fairbanks wed,
And many gossip columns fed.
In lavish style they cut a dash
And made, and spent, a lot of cash.

A rambling mansion was the scene
Where they both reigned like King and Queen.
Pickford and Fairbanks thought they'd let it
Be called the name of PICKFAIR — get it?!

And still the audiences raved
For Mary in the roles they craved:
So impish, innocent, demure —
A Pollyanna, sweet and pure.
Mary was typecast, to her rage,
And frozen at that girlish age.

She said: "I'll show they've had their day,
These simpering maidens I portray —
I'll get my ringlets cut away!"

She did — and if you want to see 'em,
They're in a Hollywood museum.

Mary Pickford still survived
When talking pictures first arrived.
An early Oscar she would get
To praise her acting in *Coquette*.

Mary was nearly forty now,
And soon she made her final bow.
A Western was the last we'd see
Of her, in 1933.

At Grauman's Theater, where stars went
To put their prints in the cement,
Smaller than any, Mary's pair
Of tiny hands are frozen there:
Memorials to Gladys Smith,
Canadian cinematic myth.

TRANSLATION:
"AND YOU'LL FIND MY HOME PAGE ON THE NET AT: www.guglielmomarconi.com..."

MARCONI

GUGLIELMO MARCONI   (1874 – 1937)

Marconi pioneered the development of radio, and made many of his key experiments in Canada. He won the Nobel Prize in 1907.

Marconi from his youth was tireless
In his experiments with wireless.
He thought he'd see his methods score
In messages from ship to shore.

His Government told poor Marconi
That all his schemes were pure boloney.
To England then Marconi came
And there began to make his name.
On lightships soon his gear was placed
And also used when yachts were raced.

Then Queen Victoria thought she might
Install it on the Isle of Wight.
She said: "My son the Prince of Wales
With riotous parties often sails.
Now I can learn, by dash and dot,
Just what he's up to, on his yacht."

And now Marconi had his eyes
Upon an even bigger prize.
He told investors: "I've a notion
To signal right across the ocean."
They knew that he was not a quitter,
And so they backed his new transmitter.

He built it very near Land's End
And got it all prepared to send,
But knew that no one would believe it
Until he'd somewhere to receive it.

In Newfoundland he built a station
To hear that first communication.
The aerial wire was quite a sight:
It was two hundred yards in height
And was suspended from a kite.

The first wire snapped — the second try
Rose up triumphant in the sky.
Marconi went indoors to hear,
And stuck the earphone in his ear.

He listened, worried, for a while,
Then gave a wide Italian smile.
He cried: "I hear it! Yes, yes, yes —
It's DOT-DOT-DOT — the letter S!
Wireless is here to stay, of course,
Thanks to myself, and Signor Morse.
The future beckons us: avanti!
We'll go and open the chianti!"

But cable companies with clout
Wanted to throw Marconi out.
Their plan, so grasping, vile and sinister,
Was foiled by Canada's Prime Minister.

Sir Wilfred Laurier said: "OK,
You may continue in Glace Bay,
And we shall put some funds your way."

So there on Nova Scotia's shore
More great successes lay in store.
The Governor-General released
The first transmission west to east.
Marconi then with joy was frantic,
For he had spanned the north Atlantic.
Soon many messages would fly
Thousands of miles across the sky.

And Canada he'd always thank
For seeing his intellectual rank,
When others thought him just a crank
And could not understand just what
Would come of that first DOT-DOT-DOT.

MARSHALL McLUHAN   (1911 – 1980)

Marshall McLuhan spent most of his academic life at the University of Toronto, but he gained world-wide renown with his witty and provocative pronouncements on all aspects of the modern media and popular culture.

The schools of Manitoba nourished
The young McLuhan, and he flourished.
At university and college
His brain absorbed prolific knowledge.

He filled his bright, capacious mind
With poetry of every kind,
Much treasure in the Bible found,
And relished Eliot and Pound.

In youth he said: "It's clear to me —
A teacher I shall never be."
But that is just what he became,
A great one, with a world-wide name.

First faced with freshmen, he'd conclude:
"I'm baffled by their attitude.
Their views, morality and such
To me are simply Double Dutch!
To understand their point of view
I must absorb their culture too."

And so began a study which
Would make him famous, praised, and rich.

He beamed his penetrating mind
On media of every kind.

The ads, the soaps, the radio,
The hit parade, the TV show,
Papers and comics, movies, sports,
Were processed in McLuhan's thoughts.

These thoughts his well-known view would presage —
He said: "The Medium is the Message."
He thought that every new variety
Of medium had changed society.

The advent of the printing press
Had made man's tribal loyalty less.
And now TV, that novel entity,
Would cause us all to lose identity.

Ads were aggressive, he opined:
Sex and technology combined.
And television was pollution —
So really, what was the solution?

We had to understand, he urged,
New media as they emerged.
The rear-view mirror showed, he said,
Only a world that's past and dead.
It's better far to look ahead.

His media studies, as they grew,
Brought *him* mass audiences too.
This academic was a wow,
A modern media guru now.
Star of the electronic age,
The Global Village was his stage.

To family life and university
He added roles of great diversity.
He flew around on lecture missions,
Advised or hectored politicians,
Wrote copious letters to his friends,
And analysed the latest trends.
He even played, to cap it all,
A walk-on part in *Annie Hall*!

The media loved him — well, they would:
For sound bites he was always good.
And many companies and firms
Would hire him, on most lavish terms,
To tell them, in his jokey way,
Their practices were all passé.

He said that books, however pleasant,
Were now completely obsolescent.
And some asked why, since he'd so slight them,
He was continuing to write them?

Such barbs he never thought were vexing:
He'd make his answers more perplexing.
He dealt in quips and verbal shocks
And relished puns and paradox.

"Marshall," said one who held him dear,
"Likes churning up the atmosphere;
Provocative and never dumb,
He slugs his critics till they're numb."

And though his fame began to ebb,
The Internet and World Wide Web
May now revive his trenchant theories —
Perhaps they'll make a TV series,
And there McLuhan will survive
And through the Global Village drive
The Information Super Highway,
And cry: "You see — they did it *my* way!"

ROCKET RICHARD

MAURICE "THE ROCKET" RICHARD
(b. 1929)

One of fhe great hockey stars of all time, Maurice Richard played for the Montreal Canadiens for nearly twenty years, broke many records and helped the team to win eight Stanley Cups. He was so popular with the fans that his suspension once caused a riot in the city.

A Governor-General, called Lord Stanley,
Liked games that were robust and manly.
The fastest, toughest game, he thought,
Was Canada's great winter sport.

Ice hockey first began to thrive
Way back in 1855,
When someone grabbed a hockey stick
And cried: "Now, get your skates on, quick!
Though hockey on the grass is nice,
We'll play it faster on the ice."

It caught on quickly, and became
A favourite Canadian game.
Lord Stanley never ever tired
Of seeing the game he so admired.
He said: "I'd love to take it up,
But I'm an old dog, not a pup:
Instead, I shall present a Cup."

And so the Stanley Cup was made,
And for it fierce, fast games are played:
Tumultuous, titanic clashes

Where every player swerves and dashes
And swoops and darts and sometimes crashes.
Defeat and danger they defy,
Hoping to hold that trophy high.

Now, Hockey's crowded Hall of Fame
Resounds with many a famous name.
Among the greatest, many claim,
To reach the summit of the game
Rocket Richard's best of all —
Canadiens' star, in Montreal.

It was in 1942
The Rocket first soared into view,
And fans of the Canadiens
Watching him play, exclaimed: "Tiens!
Maurice va jouer très bien!"

And they were right — for eighteen years
The Forum rang with rapturous cheers
As, blazing forth in every game,
The Rocket really earned his name.

Just two years after he'd begun
The team sure made those Red Wings run:
The record score was 9 to 1.
A game to come was better still —
A play-off, won Eleven-Nil.

The Final of the Stanley Cup
In '52 lined two teams up:
Boston and Montreal were playing;
Canadiens' fans were surely praying —
They couldn't bear it if they lost on
Such a night, to rivals Boston.

Each team was full of brave defiance —
This was a battle of the giants.
The scores were even for a spell;
A heavy tackle — Maurice fell!
Knocked out and bloody, he revived —
The tie-break finally arrived.

The winning goal the Rocket scored:
Fans cheered the hero they adored.
The crowd stood up, and that ovation
Was four whole minutes in duration.

Many times since, those rival Bruins
Were left with their defence in ruins;
And there were lots of other teams
Who left the ice with shattered dreams.
Canadiens' goals inspired the Forum,
And Maurice knew just how to score 'em.

Richard his name has also lent
To one unfortunate event,

The Richard Riot, which we know
Was more than forty years ago.

A fight had happened on the ice —
Richard's behaviour wasn't nice.
Said Hockey's President: "Richard —
From all this season's games, you're barred!"

The President's decision came
The night before a Red Wings game.
The fans thought this appalling manners,
And marched the streets with protest banners.
President Campbell rashly came
To take his seat to watch the game.

The fans, who thought he was the dregs,
Threw ripe tomatoes, rocks and eggs.
By someone's fist he soon got hit,
And then a tear gas bomb was lit.
The place filled up with yellow smoke;
The crowd began to scream and choke.

The game was lost, the fans went out
And roared and raged and rushed about.
Windows were smashed, cars overturned,
Shops looted, and some buildings burned.
The rioting went on all night,
And left the city quite a sight.

Though Maurice wanted no such show
And asked for calm, on radio,
The Richard Riot always came
To be remembered with his name.

The next year, that same President
The Stanley Cup would soon present
To Maurice, for his winning team:
A nightmare turned into a dream.
And then, from there the team would go
To win four more Cups in a row.

More records saw him top the polls:
The first to get five hundred goals,
And first to score, of all great names,
His fifty goals in fifty games.
Eight Stanley Cups he helped to win;
First TV coverage he was in.

His reputation — none would knock it,
For there's been no one like The Rocket!

PIERRE TRUDEAU

PIERRE TRUDEAU
(b. 1919)

Flamboyant Montreal lawyer Pierre Trudeau became Prime Minister in 1968 and led the country for most of the following sixteen years, during which he was both idolized and reviled, but never ignored.

Cultured and cool and charismatic,
Pierre's career was never static.
One of the Liberals' leading lights,
He led them up towards the heights;
Then as he basked upon the summit,
His popularity would plummet.
And when it looked like he'd been trounced,
Back to the top he promptly bounced.

Pierre grew up in Montreal;
A schoolboy essay he'd recall:
"What do you want to be?" He thought:
Seaman...? Explorer...? Astronaut...?
(They'd laugh if he had written: "I've
A plan to move to Sussex Drive.")

But Law was what he wound up doing,
And on vacations, went canoeing.
The doctorate plans which he unfurled
Meant travelling around the world —
And so with backpack and with beard
The Hippie Trail he pioneered,
And foiled a knife attacker's bid

While climbing up a Pyramid.
(A useful skill in later life
In worlds where back-stabbing is rife.)

Back home, he saw the great appeal
Of *Révolution Tranquille*.
The Liberal Party wooed him then
As one of Québec's Three Wise Men.
So, somewhat to his own surprise,
Began his meteoric rise.

Just two years after his election
He stood for leadership selection.
The Old Guard said: "He'll cause us scandals —
The guy wears coloured shirts, and sandals!
Voters will never choose Pierre —
They'd rather have a grizzly bear!"

But they were wrong, that diehard band,
For Trudeaumania swept the land.
It gave the party such a boost,
Soon Pierre Trudeau ruled the roost.
It was the Liberals' finest hour:
The red rose had begun to flower.

The Right looked on with some anxiety
As Trudeau launched his Just Society.
He then said: "Though you may berate us,

We're giving French official status.
The Anglophones must mend their ways
And recognize La Langue Française."

It's no surprise the Opposition
Did not share Trudeau's sense of mission.
He called them "nobodies", a phrase
They hardly took as lavish praise.

One day he mouthed a certain word
In mime, so it could not be heard.
When asked, so there should be no muddle,
What was it? He said: "Fuddle Duddle!
Or really racily, it may be
I *might* have told you, Fuddle Dee Dee!"

For sixteen years Pierre would reign,
Although his star would wax and wane.
Once, when faintly it did burn,
For nine months, Joe Clark took a turn.

Pierre was showy and dramatic,
Though critics called him autocratic.
"His style," said one, "though he's a stayer,
Makes Judas seem a good team player."

But now and then he got it wrong
With slogans like THE LAND IS STRONG,

To which the voters, like as not,
Were apt to yawn and say: "So what?"

Advisers, in his third campaign,
Said: "Margaret, please don't join the train."
That view she said she would defy;
She called Pierre a loving guy,
And crowds all cheered her to the sky.
But politics would take their toll —
She'd go elsewhere to rock and roll.

Pierre's career went rolling on;
Sometimes he struggled, sometimes shone.
Once, in a ploy both cute and neat,
He engineered his own defeat,
Another time resigned, and then
Decided to come back again.

His progress sometimes could be chequered,
And very nearly got Quebecer'd.
He found it hard to keep in check
The separatists in Quebec,
Tried to maintain a plural nation
And keep them in the Federation —
While other provinces, no doubt,
Were quite inclined to boot them out.

But he survived, to sweat and toil
To solve the crisis over oil,

And eat his words, and eat them whole,
On needs for wage and price control.

But Trudeau, still the clever mover,
The Gang of Eight would outmanoeuvre
And greet with triumph and elation
The Constitution's patriation.

He thought he'd closed that "can of worms",
And later spoke in scathing terms
Of those who opened it to make
Supposed improvements at Meech Lake
And an Accord at Charlottetown.
But then the voters turned them down.

Whether Pierre was loved, or hated,
His style was never understated.
And round the world as he gyrated,
He made quite sure, when he was fêted,
That Canada was highly rated.

Pierre's one of the brighter gems
In lists of Canada's P.M.'s.
Sir John MacDonald was the first —
A great man, with a greater thirst.
He found at last he couldn't handle
The great Pacific Railway scandal.

Then came Mackenzie (Alexander)
A man who was immune to slander.

Translating Gettysburg's Address
Was Wilfrid Laurier, no less —
Abe Lincoln he admired, we knew,
And much admired the ladies too.

The twentieth century would bring
William Lyon Mackenzie King:
The longest serving leader, he
Had one great eccentricity,
For by Ouija board he tried
To reach folks on the Other Side;
His mother, so he claimed, replied.

And then there was rumbustious Dief,
Conservatives' impressive Chief.
Stanfield and Meighen and Joe Clark
To lead the country would embark.
Each made a great or lesser mark.

Lester Pearson did so well,
He got the Peace Prize from Nobel.
From him the leadership would go
Eventually to Pierre Trudeau.

Then Brian Mulroney wheeled and dealed
And quite a fashion sense revealed.

And for a short while, after him,
We caught the briefest glimpse of Kim.

Jean Chrétien took up the fight —
He was a Trudeau acolyte,
So once again the torch could flare
In tribute to the great Pierre!

SASQUATCH

SASQUATCH

The Sasquatch, also known as Bigfoot, is a tall hairy creature believed to inhabit the mountains and forests of the Canadian and American northwest. Many sightings have been reported and many footprints found, but scientists are still not certain whether the Sasquatch and its similar Himalayan counterpart, the Yeti, are mythical or real.

The Sasquatch, so the story goes,
Has long arms, and a wide, flat nose.
He walks tall — there's no doubt of that —
He's nine feet high, without a hat.

Though tales of his appearance vary,
They all agree he's very hairy.
His four-foot chest is like a wall,
He seems to have no neck at all:
In fact, his build would make him seem
A natural for the football team.

His big toe's huge, his feet the same;
No wonder, when he rose to fame,
That BIGFOOT was his other name.

In folklore, though it's hardly science,
He is descended from the Giants
Who fought in two ferocious bands
Among the northwest forest lands.
Their gentler offspring, legends say,
Roam in those mountain woods today.

Some claim he's cousin to the Yeti
Whose footprints, scattered like confetti,
Make disbelief seem simply petty.
But skeptics still maintain that no men
Have *seen* Abominable Snowmen.

The Bigfoot Sasquatch, though, has been
By many different people seen.
Even a film for one whole minute
Has claimed to have the creature in it.
This claim some scientists refute
And say the figure, though hirsute,
Is someone in a monkey suit.

Earlier, miners in a shack
Claimed they'd been subject to attack.
When skeptics said, once more aloof:
"If that's a Sasquatch, where's the proof?"
The miners growled: "Then *who*, you goof,
Spent all night pounding on the roof?"

One Albert Ostman claimed that he
At Toba Inlet, in B.C.,
Was kidnapped by a family.
One night when he was camping out
A giant Sasquatch lurked about,
And gathered up his gear, then crept
And picked up Ostman as he slept.

He took him home to meet the wife,
And Ostman shared their Sasquatch life.
Their son and daughter too were there:
The captive was a sight so rare
They never ceased to laugh and stare.

Although they offered him no harm,
He found the life had little charm.
He slipped away into the distance —
At least he'd proof of their existence!
The only proof, though, was *his* word,
And few believed in what they heard.

In spite of countless sightings more
And sets of prints of feet galore
The skeptics say that these alone
Are not enough, just on their own.
They say that not one hair or bone
Or even tooth has once been shown.

So where have all the Sasquatch gone?
The controversy rages on.
Are Yetis, Bigfoots, and Sasquatches
Seen only after several scotches?

Are they as fictional as Chaucer,
Or creatures from a Flying Saucer?
And more believable or less
Than Monsters living in Loch Ness?

Perhaps they're prudently deciding
It's safer if they stay in hiding.
Who wants to be coralled in zoos,
Or pictured on the TV News?

Perhaps the truth we'll never know.
There's one big question lurking, though:
However *we* may fret and fuss,
Do Sasquatches believe in *us*?

OH, CANADIANS!

AUTHOR'S NOTE

I was both delighted and daunted when Kim McArthur, President o
Little, Brown Canada, asked me to write this book. Kim had enjoyed the
satirical verses I'd written about characters in English history, ranging
from King Henry VIII to Agatha Christie. Why not, she said, give the
same treatment to some of Canada's famous figures?

For several months the study in our Dublin home where Maeve and
I work was piled with books — and maps too, to trace the journeys of
all those explorers who set out to find the Northwest Passage to the
Pacific, and ended up somewhere quite different.

I enjoyed the research and the writing, and was most impressed with
the imagination and tenacity, and sometimes the fine eccentricity, of the
variety of people who helped to shape Canada's history.

I am very grateful for Marsha Boulton's entertaining accounts of the
Canadian heritage in her book *Just a Minute*, and I also want to thank
the celebrated London Library off Picadilly, and the Canadian Embassy
in Dublin, for their help with research material.

Finally, I am hugely indebted to Aislin for providing such wonderful
and hilarious illustrations for the book.

Gordon Snell

The typeface used in this edition is Palatino, horizontally compressed to 85%; the book was set and electronically composed by Michael P. Callaghan, on behalf of Moons of Jupiter, Inc., at 134 Eastbourne Avenue, Toronto, Canada.